ELECTRIC LOCOMOTIVES ON SCOTTISH RAILWAYS

Colin J. Howat

AMBERLEY

First published 2018

Amberley Publishing
The Hill, Stroud
Gloucestershire, GL5 4EP

www.amberley-books.com

Copyright © Colin J. Howat, 2018

The right of Colin J. Howat to be identified as
the Author of this work has been asserted in
accordance with the Copyright, Designs and
Patents Act 1988.

ISBN 978 1 4456 7634 0 (print)
ISBN 978 1 4456 7635 7 (ebook)

British Library Cataloguing in Publication Data.
A catalogue record for this book is available from
the British Library.

Origination by Amberley Publishing.
Printed in the UK.

Introduction

Electric Locomotives on Scottish Railways covers virtually the whole of the electrified network across Scotland. The first electrification here took place on the north side of Glasgow from 1960 when the Airdrie to Helensburgh line and branches in between were done. This was followed closely by the south side of Glasgow when electrification spread to the Cathcart Circle, Neilston and Newton areas in 1962. In 1967, the lines between Glasgow Central and Gourock, along with the Wemyss Bay branch, were added to the system. Progress throughout the Central Scotland area has been steady since, with approximately 40 per cent of the whole network having now been electrified. This book covers electric locos from humble Class 81s up to and including Class 92s with images from 1974 until the present day. I have also included shots of the APT (Class 370) and Virgin Class 390s (Pendolino) as they show the further development of the original AC locomotives. Technically the APT and Virgin Pendolinos are electric multiple units (EMUs), but I have included them as most people regard them as electric locos within a powered unit.

The AC electric loco fleets are not among the most popular to have operated over Scottish metals but, like some of the contemporary diesel classes, have played a major role in developing the modernisation of the rail system. The 100-strong first generation of AC electric locomotives came from five construction groups. All were built to a common design theme stipulated by the British Transport Commision (BTC) design panel. Originally classified as AL1–AL5, the fleets were later classified 81–85 and were the backbone of the modernised electric Scottish routes until AL6 (Class 86) locomotives emerged in the mid-1960s. The first generation fleets were not without operational problems and I feel that if it had not been for the extension of the WCML electrification to Glasgow Central in 1974, some would certainly have been withdrawn much earlier than they were.

Preservation of AC electric locomotives is far from easy, with little or no chance of having an operational loco with the 25 kV AC overhead power equipment required. However, a representative of each of the pioneering classes has been saved from the breaker's yard and these are currently under the custodianship of the AC Electric Loco Group, based at Barrow Hill. Of these, the preserved Class 84 is part of the National Collection. As part of the 1955 BTC railway Modernisation Plan, it was announced by the government that all future electrification projects would be standardised on the industrial frequency 25 kV AC system. This included the Glasgow suburban lines on both the north and south side of the Clyde. In terms of locomotives a new mixed traffic standardised design was to be established. This was aimed to give uniformity in a number of areas, including driving cab layout and driving techniques. At the design stage it was agreed that the UK loading gauge was too restrictive and, therefore, electrical infrastructure clearances required a two-voltage system to allow electric train operations in tight tunnel clearance areas. A reduced voltage was therefore agreed, being at a quarter of 25 kV at 6.25 kV. However, this stipulation made it necessary to install voltage detection and voltage changeover equipment. Sections of the catenary were energised at different voltages or supplied from different feeder stations. The pantographs on electric locos and EMUs, however, could run under a continuous wire system, including neutral sections at the join of supply sections or a voltage change.

A receiver on the locomotive was detected by a trackside magnet on the approach to a neutral section running off power and locking out the power circuits for the duration of the pass through the section. The power circuits were returned to operation by another trackside magnet at the end of the neutral section. When it was time to place orders for the first generation of AC electric locos, there was no like equipment from which to draw design and technical experience. Therefore, in association with the UK traction industry (mainly AEI), the BTC chose DC traction motors fed from AC/DC conversion rectifiers. The mechanical design of the AC loco fleet came from various directives by the BTC and the Design Group within the BTC, with major input coming from industrial design companies. Some major limitations were imposed, leading to severe constraints on manufacturers' design freedom. The restrictive UK loading gauge was the main one, but other stipulations included a need for 48-inch diameter wheels, a flat lower roof to house pantographs and a 20-ton maximum axle load. This produced a range of locos with a strong family resemblance. All had standard driving cabs, most used the same auxiliary equipment and as result performance of each class was very similar. At an early stage in the design process, weight calculations showed that axle loadings could be well exceeded, and this led to a considerable redesign to equipment, delaying deliveries of all locos. All the early AC locos had bogie frame mounted traction motors, which required flexible drives to keep the unsprung weight on the axles to a minimum.

All the modern electric locos in the early 1960s, with the exception of E3055, had the same pantograph design – a Stone Faiveley unit, which was a modified version of a design used on the French railways (SNCF). Two pantographs were fitted to each loco with a contact pressure of 20 lb. The raising and lowering of the pantograph was by an air motor operated by the driver; the lifting speed controlled the impact of the pantograph with the wire. Lowering of the pantograph was done quickly to reduce the possibility of an arc, with an air cushion indicating the speed before coming to rest.

Although the orders for the first 100 locomotives were placed in the mid-1950s, design and construction was very slow, with the first locos not being delivered until between 1959 and 1964. New maintenance facilities were built at various locations including Crewe and Manchester Longsight. This was a basic depot with only two usable roads. Liverpool Allerton was also opened in the early 1960s but this did not have any permanent loco allocations. By far the largest depot was at Willesden in North London. This opened in 1965 and for many years was the hub of AC loco operations. Originally it was proposed that an AC loco facility was to be opened in Birmingham, in the Soho area. This was never built, but was subsequently developed as an EMU facility. A depot at Rugby was also opened but never fully utilised for AC locos. Shields Depot on the south side of Glasgow opened for mainly Class 303 and 311 maintenance and later took over the Class 81 locos from January 1975. As more drivers were required to handle the expanding AC loco fleet, a state of the art driver simulator was opened at Willesden in 1965. This consisted of a cab mock-up with AL1–5 type controls. It also had a moving display of the line ahead, which included signals in a basic form.

The Class 81 locos were the first production overhead electric class to commence delivery. In common with the first generation AC electric locos, voltage selection equipment for 6.25 kV and 25 kV operation was fitted. However, it was never used and was quickly removed. The Class 81s suffered from body lean caused by faults in the body support springs. This resulted in excessive lateral movement, causing the loco body to make contact with the rubber bogie lateral stops. Various modifications were carried out to reduce this problem.

However, a high number of complaints were received from drivers about bad riding and this resulted in test runs between Glasgow Shields Depot and Beattock in the winter of 1977. This resulted in a further batch of modifications to reduce lateral movement and bounce. From the early 1970s the Class 81 fleet was fitted with BCF fixed fire extinguishers as well as a battery isolation switch located on the exterior of the locos. The Class 81s remained in service on the WCML until 1991 when the remaining handful were withdrawn. The very first electric loco, E3001, was handed over to BR at Sandbach station in November 1959. At one time BR considered re-allocating the Class 81s to the Eastern Region to work between London Liverpool Street and Ipswich but this was abandoned due to the bad riding qualities of the locos.

The single largest class of electric locomotive ever ordered in the UK was the AL6, later known as Class 86. Ordered in the early 1960s, this class followed the same principle of design as the earlier class 81–85s. After initial riding problems at high speed a massive rebuilding programme was instigated in the early 1970s, which culminated in revised bogie springing. They were the mainstay of the WCML until they were replaced by the later Class 87 and 90 locos.

Following electrification of the Anglia Main Line to Norwich, the Class 86 fleet became the regular power for the London Liverpool Street to Norwich route under both BR and privatisation. The freight sector took over a considerable number of Class 86s, mainly operating for Rail Express Systems (RES), and later English Welsh & Scottish Railway (EWS) and Freightliner. By 1966 the standard BR rail blue was adopted. By 2008 only a handful of the original 100 Class 86 locos remained on the UK rail network. Class 86s proved more reliable and easier to maintain than the earlier classes. Nevertheless, problems were encountered with bogies and rough riding, which brought many complaints from crews. The hydraulic dampers on the primary suspension were partly responsible for the problems and experience showed that the systems employed on earlier classes were not suitable at high speeds. Dampers with symmetrical characteristics in bump and rebound were required and in 1968 tests were undertaken with modified dampers that improved ride quality. The Class 86s also suffered from the use of axle-hung traction motors with high unsprung weights at high speed operation. This was found to be damaging to the track, resulting in a spate of broken rails that were attributed to the impact of the locos. The exact cause of the rail damage and cracking was not fully known. For part of the track damage test programme, BR Research, in conjunction with the LM Civil Engineers Department, constructed a special dipped rail joint just north of Cheddington, and Class 81–85 locos were also run over the same track. From these tests it became apparent that a different traction motor suspension for the 86s was desirable. An interesting development was the fitting of multiple control and TDM push-pull equipment.

In the late 1980s and early 1990s, a number of Class 86/4s were dedicated to freight traffic. As a result these locos had their train heating isolated, vacuum brakes removed and the top speed reduced to 75 mph. The Class 86/6 subclass was introduced from 1989 for freight-only operation.

When originally built, the early examples were finished in electric blue, the first handful without yellow warning panels which were soon added. The first new livery to appear was in 1984 with the unveiling of the InterCity business sector, which was grey and white with red body stripes. This was subsequently followed by several variations, ending in the standard InterCity Swallow livery in 1989. The Railfreight sector introduced a new two-tone grey livery in 1986 followed by the revised Railfreight distribution colours from 1992. This was replaced by RES livery from 1993. Following rail privatisation in 1996, locos operated by Virgin West Coast services and Cross Country were quickly repainted in the red/grey house colours of Virgin. Those allocated to the Anglian route were repainted in turquoise while members of the Freightliner Group were painted green. A handful of locos emerged in EWS red and gold.

Structural modifications to the fleet have been minimal since introduction. The original four-character route indicator displays were dispensed with in the mid-1970s. Initially all were wound to four zeros. These boxes were later plated over and a pair of high intensity marker lights inserted. Headlights on all electric locos became standard from the mid-1980s.

The operating area for Class 86s had been restricted mainly due to the limits of electrification. However, as the electrified network spread and expanded in 1973 from Carlisle to Glasgow Central, 86s started to spread further north. With the electrification of the East Coast Main Line (ECML) between 1985 and 1990, the class made various appearances visiting Edinburgh on the newly electrified route from Carstairs. On the West Coast Main Line (WCML), 86s remained in charge of main line services from the days of British Rail right through to privatisation and operation by Virgin Trains. The Class 87 electric locos, or Electric Scots as they were originally termed, were ordered and built by British Rail in partnership with GEC traction at BREL Crewe. This fleet, along with Class 81–86 locos, became the prime power for the WCML from May 1974. Soon after introduction, BR relaxed the ban on naming locos and all these locos received nameplates very quickly. They remained at the forefront along with Class 90s until Virgin Trains replaced them with Class 390 Pendolinos. After this some of the Class 87s were given new leases of life by being exported to various other European countries, working with companies such as the Bulgarian operator BZK.

The Class 90s were originally ordered as a replacement for the WCML Class 87s for use on both passenger and freight work. Their superior traction characteristics saw the fleet become an immediate success. With Virgin introducing Class 390 Pendolinos from 2004, fifteen Class 90s were transferred to Anglia and worked services out of Norwich and Ipswich to London Liverpool Street. The remainder of this fleet was divided between EWS and Freightliner. Most are still used today on sleeper and freight work and continue to play a vital part in the UK railway scene.

The Class 92s were specifically built for use through the Channel Tunnel on both passenger and freight workings. As time progressed, many were to be used on the proposed overnight passenger services to use the Channel Tunnel, which included an overnight service from Glasgow Central to France and Belgium. Sadly these overnight services were never to operate. Some major changes to the order and build project were then required as BR at the time was legally prevented from selling new locos to other organisations. An umbrella organisation was set up to supply locos to different rail operators and this process became known as 'novation'. This did not, however, alter the responsibilities of the already appointed Railfreight Class 92 project team, but did generate a huge amount of extra paperwork. In May 1994, as part of the pre-privatisation split of the UK railways, European Passenger Services was separated from BR and thus another novation was needed to build and supply their locos. After all three parties agreed on one common fleet design, forty-six Class 92s were ordered, valued at around £144 million. The split was for thirty to go to Railfreight UK, nine for SNCF France and seven for European Passenger Services. To meet the very strict operating requirements for the Channel Tunnel, ensuring that trains could exit the tunnel even following failure, each loco was virtually two locos in a common body with all systems replicated.

The contract to build Class 92s was eventually awarded to Brush Traction with ABB Transportation of Zurich becoming the main sub-contractor. The first Class 92 bodyshell was delivered to Loughborough in mid-1992, where a significant level of structural testing was carried out before internal assembly commenced. The fleet build project continued until mid-1996. The formal handover of the first delivered loco came in March 1994, when a high-profile event was staged inside the main erecting shop at Brush Loughborough, with No. 92003 *Beethoven* being handed over to Railfreight Distribution. Deliveries of Class 92 bodyshells continued and by July 1994 the first of the build were at the Velim test track in the Czech Republic. Here locos were subjected to extremes of both high and low temperatures to calculate performance. The tests revealed some modifications were needed in the vent systems.

November 1994 was a significant date as a Class 92 powered a train on a UK main line for the first time when No. 92003 with No. 92018 worked a departmental train between Carnforth and Carlisle, and in appalling weather tackled the Shap incline for the first time. By the end of December that year, Class 92 locos were deemed good enough to work test trains on their own. No. 90020 was handed over to European Passenger Services (EPS) at Crewe and was subsequently transferred to the North Pole Depot. At this stage it was still the intention of EPS to use Class 92s between Waterloo International station and Calais Fréthun using Nightstar sleeper stock.

Between January and February 1995 overnight testing was conducted with various Class 92s through the Channel Tunnel as part of the certification process. By July 1996 UK safety approval had been granted for Class 92s to enter revenue-earning service. However, the first use of a Class 92 on a passenger service did not come until 12 July 1997 when No. 92030 operated a Hertfordshire Railtours Special from London to Kent. Between 1996 and 2000, the remaining members of the fleet were commissioned and made operational and based at Crewe Electric Depot. Thus, locos Nos 92020/021/032/040/044–046 were redundant before they had even carried out any work. These locos were put up for sale in 2000 but no buyers could be found, so the fleet was decommissioned and stored at Crewe. The French-owned locos were also put up for sale, but again no buyer could be found.

The Channel Tunnel operator Eurotunnel was keen to enter the freight business in both France and the UK as an open access operator and by 2010 had purchased eleven locos. In July 2011 it was announced that the remaining SNCF locos were being purchased by Europort 2/GBRf, giving GBRf a fleet of sixteen locos. However, many of these locos were in need of overhaul. The other thirty Class 92s originally owned by BR Railfreight were transferred on privatisation to EWS and became part of that fleet.

Capacity on High Speed 1 (HS1), linking London with the Channel Tunnel, was such that freight traffic could be accommodated, especially at night, but for this to happen the Class 92s had to receive major upgrading of the in-cab signalling equipment. This was progressively done from 2009, with the first train operated over HS1 being headed by a Class 92 in March 2011. By November 2011 a timetabled service was introduced, linking London Barking with Poland using European-sized wagons. The 92s operated as far as Calais Fréthun.

When they came out in the beginning, Class 92 locos were finished in Railfreight two-tone grey livery offset by a dark blue roof. As the fleet was dedicated to Channel Tunnel operations, three O-shaped tunnel segment shapes of decreasing size were applied on the bodysides, and each loco received a cast Crewe depot logo on the non-driving side. The SNCF locos' motif was applied on the driving cabside while Eurostar/EPS locos had an attractive EPS logo applied in the same position. The Railfreight batch carried cast BR double arrow badges. Some UK locos later received Railfreight Distribution branding with a Railfreight Distribution badge being applied to the bodyside. Upon privatisation and sale of the UK freight business to EWS, the company started to apply its animal logo on the bodyside of the 92s, with just two locos, Nos 92001 and 92031, receiving full maroon livery with full yellow ends. The Channel Tunnel segment badges were retained with transfer names now applied in white.

After DB Schenker, most of the Class 92 fleet is now operated by DB Cargo. A number have also been exported to Eastern Europe, where there is a large demand for powerful electric locos. Some of the fleet are also owned by GB Railfreight and have been used on internal UK sleeper services. With protracted delivery of the Class 92s in the mid-1990s, EWS at the time was forced to hire in French locos from SNCF, but by 2009 the requirement for these locos had fallen away. Today we should be thankful for the dedication of the Barrow Hill-based AC Locomotive Group as one example of each of the pioneering classes AL1–AL5 (Classes 81–85) has been saved. Preservation commenced many years before the AC Group took over and, in the main, Pete Waterman was instrumental in saving many examples from scrap. I have also been amazed by the silence of the electric loco. The early electric loco classes were quite noisy but from the Class 90s onwards were very silent. One of my best journeys was behind a Class 81 (which was being utilised in place of a failed Class 87) between Carlisle and Glasgow Central in 1981. We arrived at our destination bang on time. Fortunately, examples of the early electric locos are preserved at the roundhouse at Barrow Hill, near Staveley in Derbyshire.

Scottish electrification began during the 1960s as part of the BR 1955 Modernisation Plan. Electrification was sporadic and to this day is still incomplete. Work in Scotland began in the north side of Glasgow in 1961 on the line from Helensburgh Central in the west to Airdrie in the east, including the branches to Balloch, Springburn and Bridgeton Central. The next scheme was on the south side on the Glasgow Central to Neilston, Cathcart Circle and Newton lines in 1963. Following on from this the Glasgow Central to Gourock and Wemyss Bay lines were electrified in 1967. The UK government then gave the go-ahead for the electrification of the WCML from Preston to Glasgow Central and this was completed in 1973, with services between Glasgow Central and London Euston commencing from May 1974. In conjunction with this, the Hamilton Circle line from Newton and the Belshill route to/from Motherwell were also electrified. Next on the list was the Argyle Line between Kelvinhaugh Junction in the west and Rutherglen Central Junction in the east, which allowed the through running of trains between the south and north side of Glasgow. This also included a small spur at Rutherglen West Junction, which allowed trains direct access from the Argyle line to the WCML and thence direct access to/from Shields Depot.

In 1986 the Ayrshire area was added to the electrified network when the overheads were extended from Paisley Gilmour Street to Ayr, Largs and Ardrossan Harbour. However, in one of the most short-sighted decisions made by BR and Strathclyde PTE, the trackbed beyond Paisley Canal was lifted and houses were allowed to be built on it. This has made it virtually impossible to re-open services to/from Kilmacolm. However, given the amount of houses that were repossessed for the re-opening of the Waverley route to Tweedbank, nothing is impossible. Another part of the Scottish network added in was the Whifflet spur, which allows trains to run from Motherwell onto the North Electric system. This was used extensively from December 1994 until December 1995 after the Argyle Line was shut due to severe flooding. The Larkhall branch was added in 2005 and the R&C line from Rutherglen to Whifflet via Mount Vernon was also electrified in 2014. The E&G line between Glasgow Queen Street and Edinburgh was finally opened up for electrics in

December 2017. On the East Coast Main Line, the Edinburgh to Berwick-upon-Tweed line was electrified in 1989. This included the North Berwick Branch, and in 1991 the line between Midcalder Junction and Carstairs was electrified, allowing GNER trains from London King's Cross direct access to Glasgow Central.

So what of the future? The Edinburgh to Glasgow Central via Shotts line is currently under electrification construction and is due to open to electric trains from May 2019. The current EGIP project is to extend to Stirling and Alloa. Hopefully all the Scottish main lines will also be extended to join up all the major cities from Inverness to Glasgow Queen Street and Aberdeen to Edinburgh. And what next in the Strathclyde area? Will the tentacles of electrification spread to East Kilbride, Barrhead and Kilmarnock, among others? There is good case for extending the Neilston branch to Lugton via Uplawmoor and onto Beith as the trackbed is virtually intact. Who knows, maybe common sense will prevail and the Paisley Canal to Elderslie line and Elderslie to Kilmacolm line could be added on to the electrified network.

DEPOT CODES

BN – Bounds Green London
CE – Crewe Electric
FL – Freightliner Crewe (BR)
FLT – Freightliner Crewe
GW – Shields Depot Glasgow
HQ – Headquarters (BR)
HY – Hyndland Glasgow
LO – Longsight Manchester (BR)
MA – Longsight Manchester (Virgin)
WN – Willesden London

No. 81002 (GW) arriving at Platform 11 at Glasgow Central with ECS to form the 19.30 Royal Mail service to London Euston. It was withdrawn from traffic in December 1989. This loco escaped the scrap man; at one time it was owned by Pete Waterman but eventually ended up being owned by the AC Locomotive Group and is preserved as part of the Barrow Hill roundhouse museum. (July 1979)

A Class 86 and driver at Glasgow Central await departure with a cross-country service to Birmingham. (July 1979)

No. 85008 (CE) arrives at Glasgow Central with a service from London Euston. At this time most of these services were normally in the hands of Class 87 locos. On this occasion it looks as if the 85 was deputising for a failure. Note the Class 27 on the right running around the Mark 1 stock, probably on a local service back to Carlisle via Kilmarnock and Dumfries. (October 1979)

No. 86226 *Mail* (WN) at Platform 2 at Glasgow Central with a cross-country service to Liverpool and Manchester. This loco was renamed *Charles Rennie Mackintosh* at the same station in May 1976 but was eventually withdrawn from traffic in July 2002. (July 1979)

A Class 87 rushes past Rutherglen old station. This station was closed in November 1979 when a new station situated approximately 500 yards away replaced it as part of the re-opened Argyle Line. At this time the station was still intact but it was removed by 1981. This would have been a useful back-up island platform during Argyle Line disruptions, but the authorities decided not to keep it. (November 1979)

No. 87015 (WN) at Bridge Street outside Glasgow Central with a service from London Euston. Note on the right the former Glasgow Central Signalling Centre. This was closed in 2012 and all work passed to a new Signalling Centre facility at Springburn on the north side of Glasgow. (August 1980)

No. 85016 (CE) at Glasgow Central with a cross-country service to Birmingham. This loco was renumbered 85105 in July 1989. It was withdrawn from traffic in July 1991 and was moved to MC Metal Processing at Springburn Works, Glasgow, and was cut up by July 1992. (August 1979)

An unidentified Class 87 passes Newton station with the 10.10 Glasgow Central to London Euston service. (May 1980)

No. 81016 (GW) arrives at Paisley Gilmour Street with an advertised day excursion from Gourock to Oxenholme Lake District. (May 1982)

No. 81008 (GW) stabled outside Polmadie Depot awaiting its next duty. This loco started life as E3010 and was based at Allerton Depot, Liverpool. It was then reallocated to Crewe from January 1966 before being moved onto Shields Depot in Glasgow from January 1975. It was withdrawn from traffic in March 1988 and was eventually cut up at Coopers Metals, Attercliffe, Sheffield, by November 1991. (August 1981)

An eleven-car Class 390 south of Motherwell with the 08.40 Glasgow Central to London Euston service. (March 2016)

No. 87018 *Lord Nelson* (WN) arrives at Carstairs with the 08.05 Glasgow Central to London Euston service. (August 1981)

No. 85006 (CE) and No. 86009 (WN) stabled at Mossend Yard awaiting their next turns of duty. No. 85006 started life as E3061 and was allocated to various depots until eventually transferring to Crewe Electric from May 1973. It was renumbered 85101 in June 1989 until it was withdrawn from traffic in November 1992. No. 86009 was renumbered 86409 in November 1986 and was again renumbered to 86609 in June 1989. It is still in traffic with Freightliner. (August 1981)

A Class 85 approaches Motherwell station from the south with a Birmingham New Street to Glasgow Central service. (August 1981)

No. 87012 *Coeur De Lion* (WN) arrives at Motherwell station with a Glasgow Central to Birmingham New Street service. This loco was named at Willesden Depot in May 1978. It was in service with Virgin until withdrawn in 2004, and it then worked with GBRf hauling mail trains. In 2010 it was exported to Bulgarian operator BZK. (August 1981)

No. 85011 (CE) in the Down slow line at Arkleston Junction, north of Paisley Gilmour Street, with an empty car flat train from Linwood to Mossend Yard. These car flat trains brought new cars to Linwood for onward distribution. They were diesel-hauled to/from Arkleston Loop, then electrically hauled back to Mossend Yard and onwards to the south. (August 1981)

No. 86001 (WN) at Shields Junction heading to the nearby depot for maintenance. Note a Class 126 DMU and an APT unit stabled in the depot sidings. (August 1981)

No. 86036 (WN) stabled at Polmadie Depot awaiting its next turn of duty. This loco was originally numbered E3160. Allocated to Willesden from June 1966, it was renumbered to 86436 from July 1985. It was then renumbered again in August 1989 to 86636. It was withdrawn from traffic in 2003 and scrapped at Booths of Rotherham in 2005. (April 1982)

No. 81018 (GW) at Polmadie Depot, ready to depart with ECS to Glasgow Central for a London Euston service. This loco caught fire near Rugby in September 1985 while working a freight service. It was eventually scrapped at Springburn Works by July 1992. (April 1982)

No. 86315 (WN) passes Rutherglen with the portion off a Liverpool/Manchester to Edinburgh/Glasgow Central service. (September 1980)

An unidentified Class 86 passes Newton station with a Glasgow Central to Liverpool/Manchester service. Note the buffet car immediately behind the loco. (May 1982)

No. 86039 (WN) approaches Wallneuk Junction on the approach to Paisley Gilmour Street with ECS to Gourock to form an advertised day excursion to Oxenholme Lake District. Note that the Up and Down loops on either side of this train were occupied by both empty and loaded Cartic wagons to and from Linwood loading point. (May 1982)

No. 90039 (CE) at Carstairs with the Edinburgh sleeper portion off the overnight service from London Euston. (March 2004)

No. 370006 (GW), one of the Advanced Passenger Trains (APT), is in Hyndland Loop with a passing Class 303 EMU approaching the station. The APT was on a special from Glasgow Central High Level to the Exhibition Centre, now named Finnieston. These trains had many teething problems and were eventually withdrawn from traffic in 1986. (March 1985)

The interior of one of the APT coaches. At this time the train left Glasgow Central at 07.00 and arrived in London Euston at 11.00 – a time still not beaten by today's timetabled Virgin Pendolinos. (November 1982)

No. 81006 (GW) with a collection of Class 86 and 87 locos in the engine sidings outside Glasgow Central. This was a common sight at most main line stations on the WCML until the introduction of driving van trailers (DVTs) from 1988, which reduced the need to attach/detach locos. (April 1983)

No. 86218 *Planet* (WN) is seen running light electric at Glasgow Central. It was transferred to Norwich Depot in October 1991. Withdrawn in September 2008, the loco was exported to Hungary for the operator Floyd ZRT in February 2011. (August 1979)

A Class 85 passes Shawlands station on the outskirts of Glasgow with a diverted Bristol to Glasgow Central sleeper service. This service had been diverted away from the WCML in reaction to engineering work in the Cambuslang area. (September 1983)

No. 90017 (CE) at Platform 4 at Edinburgh, having just arrived with a service from North Berwick. These locos were taken off this service and replaced by Class 322s from 2006. (August 2005)

No. 86237 *Sir Charles Halle* (WN) arrives at Carstairs with the Glasgow portion of a Liverpool/Manchester Piccadilly-bound train. The Edinburgh portion would be coupled up shortly after arrival, with a Class 47 propelling the coaches onto the rear. (April 1984)

No. 85029 (CE) rests between duties at Carstairs stabling point. This loco was withdrawn from traffic in May 1988 after catching fire near Halewood on a football special. It was cut up at Springburn Works by MC Processing by July 1993. (April 1984)

No. 87035 *Robert Burns* (WN) and No. 87027 *Wolf of Badenoch* (WN) approach Motherwell station with a steel coil train from Mossend Yard to Dee Marsh. (April 1984)

No. 86217 (WN) at Motherwell with a Birmingham New Street to Glasgow Central service. This loco was originally numbered E3177. It was renumbered to 86217 in September 1973 and to 86504 in October 1988. It was then renumbered back to 86217 in October 1989 and was named *City University* at Liverpool Lime Street station in February 1994. It was exported to Hungary in 2003. (April 1984)

Mossend Yard with Class 81, 85 and 87 locos stabled between duties. Note the condemned Class 107 DMU power car on the far left, heading south to the scrap man. (May 1982)

No. 87009 *City of Birmingham* (WN) rests between duties at Mossend Yard. It was named at Birmingham New Street in November 1977 and was withdrawn from BR service in November 2003. Eventually, in May 2012, it was exported to Bulgaria. (May 1982)

No. 81022 (GW) plus an unidentified Class 85 stabled at Mossend Yard. No. 81022 originally started as E3097. It was another loco originally allocated to Crewe Electric and moved to Shields Depot in March 1975. It was withdrawn from traffic in June 1987 after sustaining fire damage and was cut up at Crewe Works by January 1988. (May 1982)

No. 85040 (WN) approaches Glasgow Central with a service from Liverpool and Manchester. This loco was withdrawn from traffic in October 1991 and cut up at Springburn Works by January 1993. (December 1984)

No. 81012 (GW) stabled in the old Platform 11A at Glasgow Central. This platform was removed in 2010 along with the car park to create an additional platform to increase capacity in the station. This loco was withdrawn from traffic in April 1989 after suffering fire damage and was finally cut up at Coopers Metals, Sheffield, by November 1991. (December 1984)

No. 86402 (WN) arrives in Glasgow Central with a cross-country service from Birmingham New Street. This loco was originally numbered E3170, then No. 86002 from May 1973 and became No. 86402 from January 1985. It was again renumbered 86602 in November 1989. It was withdrawn from service in 2003 and scrapped at Crewe Works in 2010. (February 1985)

No. 86209 *City of Coventry* (WN) at Rutherglen with a Glasgow Central to Birmingham New Street service. This loco was derailed at Watford in January 1975 while working a Manchester Piccadilly to London Euston express. Eventually it was repaired and worked again over WCML metals until withdrawn temporarily from traffic in June 1998. It was reinstated after a few months and went to work with Anglia Railways until withdrawn in December 2003. It was scrapped at Boreham, Essex, in July 2005. (September 1980)

Above: The APT again, this time near Kelvinhaugh Junction, west of Partick, with ECS off a special on the approach to Partick, going towards Hyndland Loop to reverse after dropping its guests off at Finnieston station. (March 1985)

Left: The APT at Rutherglen West Junction, coming off the WCML to join the Argyle lines. The train ran from Glasgow Central High Level to the Exhibition Centre via the Argyle Line. (March 1985)

No. 86414 *Frank Hornby* (WN) approaches Kilwinning station with the 06.00 Glasgow Central to Ayr service. This loco is still operational as No. 86614, allocated to Crewe in the DFNC Freightliner pool and wearing their green and yellow livery. (May 1987)

No. 86230 *The Duke of Wellington* (WN) at Townhead, south of Ayr station, with ECS to form the 07.45 to London Euston via Glasgow Central service. (August 1987)

No. 90001 (HQ) at Glasgow Central with a dynamometer coach. This was a special coach used by BR to record track alignment and provide various other technical information, mainly for the benefit of the civil engineers. (March 1988)

No. 87004 *Britannia* (WN) in Glasgow Central engine sidings. This loco was taken into BR stock from July 1973 and named at Crewe station in April 1978. This loco was exported to Bulgaria in 2010. (June 1988)

A Class 81 stabled outside Shields Depot, Glasgow, awaiting maintenance. (November 1986)

No. 87022 *Cock of the North* (WN) at the buffers of Glasgow Central having just arrived with the 07.45 Ayr to London Euston service. (June 1988)

No. 90002 (WN) departs from Ayr station with ECS to Ayr Townhead after arriving with the 06.00 service from Glasgow Central. This was the first time a Class 90 had been rostered on this turn. (July 1988)

No. 86230 *The Duke Of Wellington* (WN) at Platform 9 at Glasgow Central having just arrived with a service from London Euston. (May 1988)

No. 90004 (WN) at Glasgow Central having just arrived with ECS from Polmadie Depot to form the 17.10 service to London Euston. (October 1985)

No. 85023 (CE) at Platform 11 at Glasgow Central, probably ready to head to the nearby engine sidings. This loco caught fire near Birmingham while working a Plymouth to Glasgow passenger service in September 1989. It was then sent to Springburn Works and was eventually cut up by November 1992. (June 1989)

An unidentified Class 86/4 stands at the buffers of Platform 11 at Glasgow Central after arriving with a special from London Paddington. Note the Network SouthEast coaches. (May 1988)

No. 86257 (WN) near Abington with a Poole to Glasgow Central service. This loco was named *Snowdon* at Willesden Depot in January 1981. It was broken up at Immingham TMD by November 2003. (July 1991)

No. 86101 *Sir William Stanier* (WN) at Glasgow Central with a service to Manchester. Note the Class 31 in the adjacent platform with a special. (April 1988)

No. 91012 (BN) at Carluke passes through on the rear with a Glasgow Central to London King's Cross via Edinburgh service. (July 1991)

A Class 91 on the rear of a Glasgow Central to King's Cross service departing from Carstairs. (March 2004)

No. 86255 *Penrith Beacon* (WN) arrives at Motherwell with a Glasgow Central to Paignton service. This loco was named at Penrith station in November 1980. It was withdrawn from traffic in April 1998 and was eventually moved by road to Immingham Railfreight Terminal, where it was cut up by September 2002. (July 1991)

Two Class 86 locos stabled in the west sidings at Polmadie Depot. (April 1995)

No. 86241 *Glenfiddich* (WN), stabled at Polmadie Yard awaiting its next turn of duty. This loco was named at Glasgow Central in March 1979. It was withdrawn from traffic in January 2000 and was cut up on site at Crewe Electric Depot by February 2003. (April 1995)

No. 91017 (BN) arrives at Glasgow Central with a service from London King's Cross. (September 1991)

No. 86259 *Peter Pan* (WN) shunts a Mark 2 coach at Glasgow Central. (September 1991)

No. 90011 (WN) at Glasgow Central with the 13.40 Motorail and passenger service to London Euston. Note that the loco is marshalled between the Motorail vans at the rear and the passenger coaches to the front, and is driven from the south end by a DVT. This service was withdrawn around 1996. (May 1993)

No. 87004 (WN) at Croftfoot, on the south side of Glasgow, on the rear of a diverted Glasgow Central to London Euston service. This service had been diverted due to engineering work near Newton. (January 1995)

No. 91013 (BN) approaches Shields Junction with a diverted Glasgow Central to Newcastle service. This service was routed this way due to engineering work at Eglinton Street, on the outskirts of Glasgow Central. (March 1995)

No. 86613 and No. 86607 (both FLT) pass through Carstairs with a northbound Freightliner heading from Crewe Basford Hall to Coatbridge Freightliner terminal. (March 2004)

No. 87033 *Thane of Fife* (WN) at Motherwell on the rear of a Glasgow Central to London Euston service. (July 1991)

ADB No. 968021 is seen stabled outside Shields Depot between duties. This loco was initially numbered E3038 and it was renumbered to No. 84003 in May 1972. It was converted as a mobile load bank and then became ADB No. 968021 until it was finally withdrawn in November 1985. It was taken to Vic Berry's yard, Leicester, and scrapped by February 1986. (February 1984)

Class 86 and 87 locos, plus coaches and a Class 47 in the distance, lying stabled in Polmadie Down Yard. (April 1995)

A Class 86 passes Lesmahagow Junction and approaches Motherwell station with a Glasgow Central to Manchester Piccadilly service. (February 2002)

No. 91005 (BN) at the rear of a Glasgow Central to London King's Cross service at Edinburgh. The loco was marshalled the wrong way, presumably due to an earlier failure. (February 1996)

No. 82001 (LO) near Shields Junction with a car train from Luton to Linwood, north of Johnstone. The electric worked the train as far as Paisley Loop, where a diesel then took over. This loco was withdrawn from traffic in July 1983 and scrapped at Vic Berry's of Leicester by March 1985. (August 1981)

No. 90017 (CE) with a failed No. 90026 (WN) inside arrives at Glasgow Central with the overnight sleeper from London Euston, arriving at 13.30, approximately six hours late. This loco was on display at the BR open day at Crewe Works in August 1996. It was named *Rail Express Systems* at London Euston in March 1995. (July 1998)

A Class 87 passes Mossband Level Crossing, just south of Gretna Junction, with a London Euston to Glasgow Central service. (May 1983)

No. 90020 *Sir Michael Heron* (CE) stabled in the Motorail sidings at Edinburgh. Note the Class 305 units in the background, which were in use on North Berwick duties. This loco was named in May 1997 and it is still in service with DB Cargo. (August 1998)

Edinburgh Waverley sees a Class 91 on the rear of a Leeds-bound service. Note the Class 117 DMU in the background working a Fife Circle service. (August 1998)

No. 90026 (WN) at Edinburgh Waverley, stabled between duties. This loco is still in use with DB Cargo. (August 1998)

No. 86225 *Hardwicke* (WN) arrives at Haymarket with a Virgin CrossCountry service from Edinburgh to Birmingham New Street. It was withdrawn from service in December 2002 and was scrapped at Booths of Rotherham in April 2006. (May 2000)

No. 86242 (WN) approaches Carstairs with a Glasgow Central to London Euston service. (August 1981)

A Class 86 in Platform 3 at Glasgow Central with a Virgin CrossCountry service to Poole. (May 2000)

A Class 91 at Haymarket station on the rear of a Glasgow Central to London King's Cross service. (May 2001.

No. 90026 *Crewe International Electric Maintenance Depot* (WN) at Haymarket with sleeper ECS from Edinburgh to Polmadie Depot. (November 2001)

No. 92031 *Schiller* (CE) stabled at Ayr Depot. This was an open day organised by EWS for staff and friends. This loco is still active with DB Cargo. (April 2002)

Glasgow Central engine sidings sees two Class 87s and a Class 86 awaiting their next turns of duty – a common sight until DVTs were phased in from 1988. (May 1995)

No. 86224 (WN) is seen dead inside a Virgin Class 47 passing through Kilmarnock with a diverted Glasgow Central to London Euston service. (November 1998)

No. 81008 (GW) stabled at Ayr Townhead sidings along with Class 08, 20, 26, 27 and 37 locos as part of a BR open day. Note the fish emblem on the side of the loco. (August 1985)

No. 81008 (GW) again, this time at Haymarket Depot. This loco was at the depot in conjunction with another BR open day. This loco was withdrawn from BR in March 1988; it was moved to Tinsley Yard and cut up by November 1991. (August 1985)

No. 81020 (GW) is seen receiving an examination inside its home depot of Shields. This loco was withdrawn in July 1987 after sustaining severe body corrosion. It was taken to the funeral parlour at Tinsley and was cut up by December 1991. (November 1986)

No. 81007 (GW) at Platform 3 at Glasgow Central, ready to take ECS to Polmadie Depot. This train was a cross-county service that had arrived from Manchester and Liverpool. (May 1986)

No. 92038 *Voltaire* (CE) near Abington with a northbound engineers' train from Carlisle Yard to Millerhill Yard. This loco still earns its crust with DB Cargo. (August 2014)

No. 81020 (GW) at Paisley Gilmour Street with the 07.45 Ayr to London Euston service. The loco would be detached at Glasgow Central and replaced with either a Class 86 or 87. This loco was withdrawn from traffic in September 1987. (May 1987)

No. 85012 (CE) passes Hamilton Depot on a driver trainer, running from Polmadie Depot and back via the Hamilton Circle. This loco was renumbered 85104 in June 1989 but was withdrawn from traffic in July 1991. It was moved to Springburn Works and was cut up by January 1993. (April 1982)

No. 85016 (CE) departs from Glasgow Central with a service for Birmingham New Street. This loco was withdrawn from traffic in May 1990. (April 1980)

No. 83010 (CE) arrives at Glasgow Central with ECS from Polmadie CSD to form a cross-country service to Liverpool and Manchester. (August 1979)

No. 85003 (CE) at Glasgow Central, awaiting a move to the engine sidings. This loco was renumbered to 85113 in October 1990. It was withdrawn from traffic in November 1991 and was scrapped at Springburn Works by January 1993. (May 1990)

No. 86258 (WN) passes Rutherglen Old station with a cross-country service from Birmingham New Street to Glasgow Central. The new Rutherglen station for the Argyle line is in the background. (September 1980)

No. 86315 *Rotary International* (WN) passes Mossband Level Crossing, just south of Gretna Junction, with a Blackpool to Glasgow Central relief service. (May 1983)

No. 86244 *The Royal British Legion* (WN) passes Gretna Junction with a northbound express from Liverpool/ Manchester to Glasgow/Edinburgh. (May 1983)

No. 86422 (WN) approaches Glasgow Central in the snow with a service from Liverpool and Manchester. (February 1985)

No. 86245 *Dudley Castle* (WN) at Irvine with the 07.45 Ayr to London Euston via Glasgow Central service. This loco started out as E3182 and was renumbered to 86245 in April 1974. It was withdrawn from traffic in September 2003 with traction motor problems. It was later moved to Immingham in December 2003 and was eventually scrapped by 2010. (July 1987)

No. 86426/E3195 (WN) in Caledonian blue livery at Glasgow Central having arrived with the overnight sleeper from London Euston. This loco was named *Pride of the Nation* at London King's Cross station in January 1998. It was withdrawn from traffic in September 2002 and was eventually cut up at Booths of Rotherham in September 2005. (July 1987)

A Class 87 hurtles past Carlisle Kingmoor Yard and a Class 25 with a southbound express service from Glasgow Central to Birmingham New Street. (May 1983)

No. 86230 *The Duke of Wellington* (WN) at Ayr station with the 07.45 service to London Euston. (August 1987)

No. 86413 *County of Lancashire* (WN) at Gailes, between Barassie and Irvine, with the 07.45 Ayr to London Euston via Glasgow Central service. This loco was renumbered to 86613 and is still currently working with Freightliner. (May 1990)

No. 86401 (WN) *The Chartered Institute of Transport* in Network SouthEast livery at Glasgow Central, having just arrived with ECS from Polmadie Depot. This loco was withdrawn from traffic in December 2002 and the nameplates were removed around June 2003. It is one of the few Class 86 locos to have made it into preservation and is currently owned by the AC Locomotive Group. (February 1987)

No. 86316 (WN) is seen near Gretna Junction with a southbound express from Glasgow Central to Birmingham New Street. This loco was originally numbered E3109, then became No. 86016 in September 1973 and No. 86416 in March 1987. It was in traffic until January 2004, when it was taken out of service. It was scrapped by Booths of Rotherham by July 2005. (May 1983)

No. 86033 (WN) is seen near Crawford on a northbound express. This loco was originally E3198 and was later renumbered 86033 in April 1974. It was then renumbered to 86433 in May 1985 and named *Wulfruna* at Wolverhampton station. It was renumbered again to 86633 in September 1989 and worked for Freightliner until withdrawn in February 2004. It was then moved to Crewe LNWR and was scrapped by March 2013. (September 1980)

An unidentified Class 86 departs Glasgow Central with the 19.30 mail service to London Euston. Nowadays Royal Mail traffic is mainly moved by Class 325s from Shieldmuir Depot, south of Motherwell. (May 1982)

A Class 91 stands at Haymarket station, ready to depart with a Leeds to Glasgow Central service. (August 2009)

A sight virtually not seen anymore: a Class 86 creeps up to the end platform signal, in this case Platform 2 at Glasgow Central, after an express has departed ahead. The loco would probably be stabled in the engine sidings before coming back into the station and topping another express to the south. (May 1984)

No. 85029 (CE) arrives at Kingmoor Yard, north of Carlisle, with a Speedlink service from Mossend. (February 1986)

An unidentified Class 87 crosses the Clyde near Crawford with a northbound express. (September 1985)

A Class 86 near Flemington with a Manchester Piccadilly to Edinburgh service. (February 2002)

A Class 86 in InterCity livery arrives in Edinburgh with ECS from Craigentinny Depot to form a cross-country service to Birmingham New Street via the WCML. (October 2000)

No. 86253 *The Manchester Guardian* (WN) approaches Glasgow Central with a cross-country service from Birmingham New Street. (June 2000)

No. 87035 *Robert Burns* (WN) at Glasgow Central, having just arrived with an express from the south. This loco was named at Glasgow Central in May 1974. (August 1987)

No. 90009 *The Economist* (WN)
approaches Glasgow Central
with Mark 2 coaches to form a
cross-county service to Birmingham
New Street. (June 2000)

No. 87007 *City of Manchester* (WN)
approaches Irvine with the 07.45
Ayr to London Euston via Glasgow
Central service. The siding in the
foreground was part of the former
branch to Irvine Harbour, closed in
1971. No. 87007 was withdrawn from
traffic in 2004 and later exported to
BZK in Bulgaria. (August 1987)

No. 87012 *Coeur de Lion* (WN) at
the buffers of Platform 3 at Glasgow
Central. This loco was later named
The Olympian. It was another loco
withdrawn by Virgin in 2004 and
exported to Bulgaria. (May 1984)

An unidentified Class 87 at Gailes, between Barassie and Irvine, with the 07.45 Ayr to London Euston via Glasgow Central service. (August 1987)

No. 87016 *Coeur de Lion* (WN), this time with Mark 3 coaches in InterCity livery at the buffers of Platform 11 at Glasgow Central. (August 1987)

A Class 87 passes Abington Loop with a Glasgow Central to London Euston express. Note the Class 25 in the sidings, which had failed due to a seized axle. (September 1985)

No. 87002 *Royal Sovereign* (WN) at Crawford with a southbound express. (September 1985)

No. 87023 *Velocity* (WN) at Helensburgh Central with the Royal Train. Prince Charles and Lady Diana Spencer were on a visit to the area. (November 1986)

No. 87035 *Robert Burns* (WN) at Ayr station. The loco had been sent as part of a publicity drive to promote the new Ayrshire electrification route. Note the brand-new Class 318 stabled behind the loco in the then new orange Strathclyde livery. (September 1986)

No. 87005 *City of London* (WN) sits in the Klondyke sidings at Edinburgh awaiting its next turn of duty. These sidings are known as the Klondyke because they were named after the gold rush of the 1890s in Canada. (June 1991)

No. 87004 *Britannia* (WN) arrives at Platform 1 at Glasgow Central with an express from London Euston. (August 1987)

No. 87016 *Willesden Intercity Depot* (WN) backs onto DVT No. 82138 (CE) to work a southbound express. This loco was withdrawn from traffic in 2004. (February 1998)

A Class 86 approaches Shields Junction with ECS from Polmadie CSD to Glasgow Central. The ECS had been diverted this way due to engineering work on the main line in the Eglinton Street area. Note the Class 303 EMU in the background, heading into Glasgow Central with ECS from Corkerhill CSD. (March 1995)

No. 90038 (WN) at the Motorail sidings, Edinburgh. This loco would be stabled between sleeper duties. The east end of Edinburgh is set to see major changes from 2019. (June 2004)

A Class 91 passes through Carstairs station with a Newcastle to Glasgow Central service. (March 2004)

A Class 86 approaches
Carluke station with
a postal service from
Glasgow Central to
Warrington Bank Quay.
(July 1991)

No. 87024 *Lord of the Isles*
(WN) is dead on the rear
of a diverted Glasgow
Central to London Euston
service near Auchinleck.
This loco was named at
Willesden in May 1978; it
was withdrawn from traffic
in 2004. (May 1998)

No. 90004 *City of Glasgow*
(WN) arrives at Glasgow
Central with a Virgin
set of Mark 3 ECS
from Polmadie CSD.
(October 2003)

No. 87035 *Robert Burns* (WN) arrives at Glasgow Central with a service from London Euston. (May 2000)

A Class 87 at the rear of a London Euston to Glasgow Central service near Lamington. (May 2002)

A Class 87 in Virgin livery arrives at Glasgow Central with ECS from Polmadie Depot. (June 2002)

A Class 92 near Lamington with a timber train from Arrochar to Shotton. (May 2001)

No. 90028 (WN) at Ayr Depot as part of an open day for staff and their families. Sadly, the depot closed in 2010. This loco was named *Hertfordshire Railtours* at Wabtec Doncaster in July 2003 and it is still on the books of DB Cargo. (May 1991)

No. 85005 (CE) at Polmadie Depot having just been coupled up to Mark 1 ECS stock, presumably for a Glasgow Central to Carlisle via Kilmarnock service. This loco remained in service until withdrawn in September 1989. It was scrapped at MC Metal Processing at Springburn Works, Glasgow, by January 1993. (April 1982)

No. 90027 *Allerton T&RS Depot Quality Approved* (WN) at Platform 11, having just arrived with the overnight sleeper from London Euston. This loco was renumbered to 90227 in February 2001. It was put back to No. 90027 in 2002. It is still earning its keep with DB Cargo. (May 2003)

No. 90008 *The East Anglian* (WN) is seen near Lamington with a London Euston to Glasgow Central service. This loco is still in use with Anglia Railways. (November 2001)

No. 92019 *Wagner* (CE) is seen at Abington with the northbound Tesco express from Daventry to Grangemouth. (August 2014)

No. 85032 (CE) is seen on the freight-only lines north of Kingmoor Yard with a northbound freight for Mossend Yard. (May 1983)

No. 87035 *Robert Burns* (WN) is seen at Irvine running light engine for the open day at Ayr to celebrate the new Ayrshire electrification service. (September 1986)

A Class 91 in original InterCity livery at Glasgow Central, turned the wrong way. This was probably because of an earlier failure or a defect in the first cab. (May 1992)

No. 91012 (BN) arrives at Glasgow Central with a service from London King's Cross. (May 1997)

No. 90022 *Freight Connection* (WN) departs from the sub-platforms at Edinburgh with sleeper ECS en route to Polmadie Depot, Glasgow. This loco was renumbered to 90222 in 2001 then back to 90022 in 2002. It is currently stored at Crewe Electric Depot and does not look as if it will return to revenue earning service. (April 2002)

No. 83001 (LO) and No. 87005 (WN) *City of London* are seen stabled in the Down sidings at Polmadie Depot, having arrived earlier with ECS from Carlisle. (April 1982)

No. 91024 *Reverend W. Awdry* (BN) arrives in Edinburgh with a service from Doncaster. Reverend Awdry was well-known for his railway books. He died in March 1997 at the age of eighty-five. (May 2002)

A Class 87 on the rear of a Glasgow Central to London Euston service at Motherwell station. (October 2002)

A Class 390 passes Carstairs station with a Glasgow Central to London Euston via Birmingham service. (March 2013)

An unidentified Class 87 passes Rutherglen old station with a London Euston to Glasgow Central service. (September 1980)

A Class 91 at the buffers of Platform 2 at Glasgow Central, ready to head south. (May 2002)

No. 90024 (WN) approaches Carstairs with the overnight sleeper from London Euston. No. 90039 (WN) waits to take away the Edinburgh portion. (March 2004)

A 2+9 Class 390 Pendolino approaches Glasgow Central with a service from London Euston via Birmingham New Street. (August 2009)

A Class 86 stands at Carlisle with a northbound express, while in the sidings No. 303027, formerly of Hyndland Depot, is being transferred and is on its way to Crewe Electric Depot. (August 1981)

No. 90049 (FL) at Bogside, between Irvine and Kilwinning, with a Hertfordshire railtour from Ayr to Crewe. This loco is still working for Freightliner. (August 1997)

No. 90022 *Freight Connection* (WN) awaits its next turn of duty at Platform 11 at Glasgow Central. (July 1998)

A Class 91 departs
Glasgow Central
with a service for
London King's Cross.
(April 2004)

A Class 85 at Mossband Level Crossing, near Gretna Junction, heads north with a mixed freight from Carlisle
Kingmoor Yard to Mossend Yard near Bellshill. (May 1983)

A Class 91 at the rear of the 07.00 Glasgow Central to London King's Cross departs from Edinburgh. (May 2002)

A ten-car Class 390 approaches the border with a London Euston to Glasgow Central service. (May 2013)

A Class 91 approaches Drem station with a London King's Cross to Edinburgh service. There is talk of this line being increased to four tracks to Edinburgh in the future. (June 2004)

No. 90027 *Allerton T&RS Depot Quality Approved* (CE) is seen at Musselburgh with a North Berwick to Edinburgh service. These locos were drafted in to operate this service between 2003 and 2004 due to a legal wrangle between the leasing companies and Transport Scotland. (June 2004)

A view from behind No. 90027 (CE) shortly after departing from Musselburgh station. At this time the service was driven by EWS drivers based at Millerhill and ScotRail conductors based at Edinburgh. (June 2004)

No. 91017 *City of Leeds* (BN) approaches Glasgow Central with a service from London King's Cross. (April 2005)

No. 91014 *St Mungo Cathedral* (BN) arrives at Edinburgh with a service from Leeds. (August 2005)

A Class 390 tilts well at Abington with a northbound London Euston to Glasgow Central via Birmingham New Street service. (August 2014)

No. 86438 (WN) is seen at Glasgow Central having just arrived with the overnight postal from London Euston. This loco is still employed by Freightliner. (February 1990)

No. 91101 (BN) at Haymarket station with a Doncaster to Glasgow Central service. Note the Class 170 heading into Edinburgh. (August 2009)

A Class 390 approaches Carstairs with a Glasgow Central to London Euston service. (March 2013)

No. 86218 *Planet* (WN) approaching Glasgow Central with a service from Liverpool Lime Street. (October 1983)

A Class 390 at Shieldmuir heading south with a Glasgow Central to London Euston service. (March 2016)

A Class 90 arrives in Glasgow Central with an express from London Euston. (February 1995)

A Class 87 on the WCML near Crawford heading north with an additional special from London Euston to Glasgow Central. (September 1985)

A Class 86 at Platform 9 at Glasgow Central awaits its driver with the 15.15 Glasgow Central–Manchester/ Liverpool service. (June 1981)

A Class 390 departs Glasgow Central with a service for Birmingham New Street. (October 2015)

No. 87012 *Coeur de Lion* (WN) arrives at Motherwell station with the 09.45 London Euston to Glasgow Central service. (March 1981)

A Class 85 unloads its parcels at Platform 12 at Glasgow Central while No. 303027 (GW) waits with a departure for Gourock. (May 1985)

No. 86638 and No. 86636 (both FL) are seen at Crawford with the 14.20 Coatbridge FLT to Crewe Basford Hall. Both locos remain in service with Freightliner. (August 2014)

No. 90017 (CE) stands at the buffers at Edinburgh next to the train crew depot at the east end of the station. A collection of drivers discuss their next work. (August 2005)

No. 92036 *Bertolt Brecht* (CE) approaches Carstairs with a southbound Freightliner from Coatbridge to Daventry. This loco is still currently employed by DB Cargo. (March 2004)

A Class 87 approaches Rutherglen old station with a Glasgow Central to Manchester and Liverpool service. (September 1980)

No. 90017 (WN) is seen approaching Glasgow Central with a service from London Euston. (April 1990)